HOW OLD?!

Quips and Quotes for Growing Older, Not Wiser

summersdale

HOW OLD?!

An Hachette UK Company
www.hachette.co.uk

Summersdale Publishers Ltd
Part of Octopus Publishing Group Limited
Carmelite House
50 Victoria Embankment
LONDON
EC4Y 0DZ
UK

www.summersdale.com

Printed and bound in China

ISBN: 978-1-78685-493-3

Substantial discounts on bulk quantities of Summersdale books are available to corporations, professional associations and other organisations. For details contact general enquiries: telephone: +44 (0) 1243 771107 or email: enquiries@summersdale.com.

To..............................

From...........................

You're how old?!

You know you're getting old when the candles cost more than the cake.

BOB HOPE

Old age is not so bad when you consider the alternative.

MAURICE CHEVALIER

EACH YEAR IT GROWS HARDER TO MAKE ENDS MEET — THE ENDS I REFER TO ARE HANDS AND FEET.

Richard Armour

Old age is like
a plane flying through
a storm. Once you're
aboard, there's
nothing you can do.

GOLDA MEIR

I don't want to retire.
I'm not that good at
crossword puzzles.

NORMAN MAILER

Harry insisted he was going through the 'manopause', hot flushes and all.

I am getting to an age
when I can only enjoy
the last sport left.
It is called hunting
for your spectacles.

EDWARD GREY

Old age at least gives me an excuse for not being very good at things.

THOMAS SOWELL

I knew I was going bald when it was taking longer and longer to wash my face.

HARRY HILL

WHEN YOU WIN, YOU'RE AN OLD PRO. WHEN YOU LOSE, YOU'RE AN OLD MAN.

Charlie Conerly

You only live once,
but if you do it right,
once is enough.

MAE WEST

After all these years,
it seemed Nancy
wasn't quite as excited
to see Derek as he was
to see her...

Time doth flit; oh shit!

DOROTHY PARKER

One should never make one's debut with a scandal. One should reserve that to give an interest to one's old age.

OSCAR WILDE

I ADVISE YOU TO GO ON LIVING SOLELY TO ENRAGE THOSE WHO ARE PAYING YOUR ANNUITIES.

Voltaire

Experience is a comb life gives you after you lose your hair.

JUDITH STERN

They say the first thing to go when you're old is your legs or your eyesight. It isn't true. The first thing to go is parallel parking.

KURT VONNEGUT

'I said, stop being so tight and buy a proper hearing aid!'

Wisdom doesn't necessarily come with age. Sometimes age just shows up all by itself.

TOM WILSON

The good old days
are now.

TOM CLANCY

Middle age is the awkward period when Father Time starts catching up with Mother Nature.

HAROLD COFFIN

THE OLDER A MAN GETS, THE FARTHER HE HAD TO WALK TO SCHOOL AS A BOY.

Henry Brightman

I used to think I'd like less grey hair. Now I'd like more of it.

RICHIE BENAUD

'Are you sure this is as loud as it goes?!'

Old age likes
indecency.
It's a sign of life.

MASON COOLEY

**Anyone can get old.
All you have to do is
live long enough.**

GROUCHO MARX

AGE IS SOMETHING
THAT DOESN'T MATTER,
UNLESS YOU ARE A CHEESE.

Billie Burke

You can't turn back the clock. But you can wind it up again.

BONNIE PRUDDEN

I just tell people I'm as old as my wife. Then I lie about her age.

FRED METCALF

Roger thought there was nothing wrong with dressing smartly to fetch the morning paper.

Always do sober what you said you'd do when you were drunk. That will teach you to keep your mouth shut!

ERNEST HEMINGWAY

Eventually you will reach a point when you stop lying about your age and start bragging about it.

WILL ROGERS

Don't worry about avoiding temptation. As you grow older, it starts avoiding you.

ANONYMOUS

LIFE IS JUST ONE GRAND, SWEET SONG, SO START THE MUSIC.

Ronald Regan

The three stages of man: he believes in Santa Claus; he does not believe in Santa Claus; he is Santa Claus.

ANONYMOUS

Take up cooking, the wife said. It's a safe midlife crisis hobby, she said.

When they tell me
I'm too old to do
something, I attempt
it immediately.

PABLO PICASSO

My doctor told me to watch my drinking, so I now do it in front of the mirror.

RODNEY DANGERFIELD

THERE'S ONE ADVANTAGE TO BEING 102. NO PEER PRESSURE.

Dennis Wolfberg

Half our life is spent trying to find something to do with the time we have rushed through life trying to save.

WILL ROGERS

Middle age is when you're old enough to know better but still young enough to do it.

OGDEN NASH

This wasn't the first time Timothy had been told he was good in the sack.

Moderation is the key to old age and the doorway to boredom.

BENNY BELLAMACINA

One of the advantages of being 70 is that you need only 4 hours' sleep. True, you need it 4 times a day, but still.

DENIS NORDEN

And in the end, it's not the years in your life that count. It's the life in your years.

ANONYMOUS

NEVER BE AFRAID TO TRY SOMETHING NEW.

Bob Hope

Not a shred of evidence exists in favour of the idea that life is serious.

BRENDAN GILL

Of course, at their age all dancing was break dancing. Last week it was an ankle.

For all the advances in medicine, there is still no cure for the common birthday.

JOHN GLENN

One of the many things nobody tells you about middle age is that it's a nice change from being young.

WILLIAM FEATHER

BY THE TIME YOU'RE 80 YEARS OLD YOU'VE LEARNED EVERYTHING. YOU ONLY HAVE TO REMEMBER IT.

Bill Vaughan

The problem with the world is that everyone is a few drinks behind.

HUMPHREY BOGART

Age is a question of mind over matter. If you don't mind, it doesn't matter!

ANONYMOUS

As the years marched on, Frederick had to put in more and more effort to ensure he still looked good in a cardigan.

Boys will be boys and so will a lot of middle-aged men.

KIN HUBBARD

Now I'm over 50 my doctor says I should go out and get more fresh air and exercise. I said, 'All right, I'll drive with the car window open.'

ANGUS WALKER

You can't help getting older, but you don't have to get old.

GEORGE BURNS

I'D HATE TO DIE WITH
A GOOD LIVER, GOOD
KIDNEYS AND A GOOD
BRAIN. WHEN I DIE
I WANT EVERYTHING
TO BE KNACKERED.

Hamish Imlach

As for me, except for an occasional heart attack, I feel as young as I ever did.

ROBERT BENCHLEY

Just checking the obituaries to see if I'm in there.

My wife said to me,
'I don't look 50,
do I darling?' I said,
'Not any more.'

BOB MONKHOUSE

As you get older three things happen. The first is your memory goes, and I can't remember the other two...

NORMAN WISDOM

FIRST, YOU FORGET NAMES, THEN YOU FORGET FACES. NEXT, YOU FORGET TO PULL YOUR ZIPPER UP.

Anonymous

A man has reached middle age when he is advised to slow down by his doctor rather than the police.

ANONYMOUS

Don't let ageing get you down. It's too hard to get back up.

JOHN WAGNER

Derek had cracked it – he could water the garden and wash the grandchildren at the same time.

Midlife crisis is that moment when you realise your children and your clothes are about the same age.

WILLIAM D. TAMMEUS

Middle age is the time when a man is always thinking in a week or two he will feel as good as ever.

DON MARQUIS

Men chase golf balls when they're too old to chase anything else.

GROUCHO MARX

THEY TELL YOU THAT YOU'LL LOSE YOUR MIND WHEN YOU GROW OLDER. WHAT THEY DON'T TELL YOU IS THAT YOU WON'T MISS IT VERY MUCH.

Malcolm Cowley

Inside every
older person is a
younger person –
wondering what the
hell happened.

CORA HARVEY ARMSTRONG

**Now, now, dear,
it happens to all men
when they reach
your age!**

Men are like wine.
Some turn to vinegar,
but the best
improve with age.

C. E. M. JOAD

Middle age is when you are not inclined to exercise anything but caution.

ARTHUR MURRAY

TO WIN BACK MY YOUTH...
THERE IS NOTHING
I WOULDN'T DO —
EXCEPT TAKE EXERCISE,
GET UP EARLY, OR BE
A USEFUL MEMBER
OF THE COMMUNITY.

Oscar Wilde

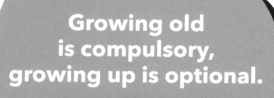

Growing old
is compulsory,
growing up is optional.

BOB MONKHOUSE

You know you've reached middle-age when your weightlifting consists merely of standing up.

BOB HOPE

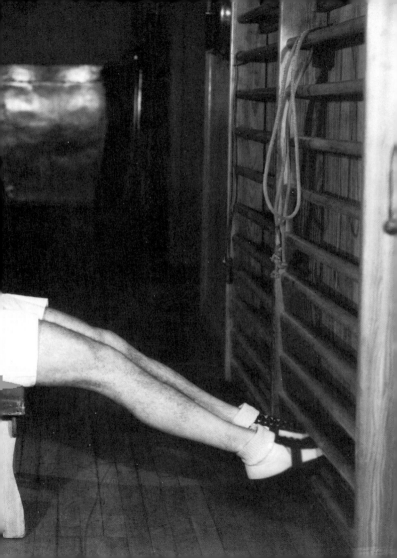

Never a tall man, Martin didn't take old-age-shrinkage very well.

When it comes to old age we're all in the same boat, only some of us have been aboard a little longer.

LEO PROBST

I have the body of
an 18-year-old. I keep
it in the fridge.

SPIKE MILLIGAN

Wrinkles should merely indicate where smiles have been.

MARK TWAIN

THEY SAY THAT AGE IS ALL IN YOUR MIND. THE TRICK IS KEEPING IT FROM CREEPING DOWN INTO YOUR BODY.

Anonymous

Getting old is a bit like getting drunk; everyone else looks brilliant.

BILLY CONNOLLY

Evenings weren't as wild as they used to be.

One day you look
in the mirror and
realise the face you
are shaving in the
mirror is your father's.

ROBERT HARRIS

Youth would be an ideal state if it came a little later in life.

H. H. ASQUITH

THE EASIEST WAY TO DIMINISH THE APPEARANCE OF WRINKLES IS TO KEEP YOUR GLASSES OFF WHEN YOU LOOK IN THE MIRROR.

Joan Rivers

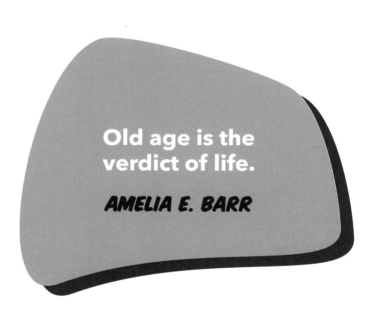

Old age is the
verdict of life.

AMELIA E. BARR

**You live and learn.
At any rate, you live.**

DOUGLAS ADAMS

When you are
about 35 years old,
something terrible
always happens
to music.

STEVE RACE

Still got it.

If you're interested in finding out more about our books, find us on Facebook at **Summersdale Publishers** and follow us on Twitter at **@Summersdale**.

www.summersdale.com